About the Author

Sharon Salomon is a lover of animals, travel, adventure and the journey of the spirit. She believes in fully loving like your heart is expanding and wrapping itself around the earth, and that if we avoid pain, we miss out on all the good bits. She lives in Johannesburg, South Africa, with her beloved canines.

Bare Skinned

Sharon Salomon

Bare Skinned

Olympia Publishers
London

www.olympiapublishers.com
OLYMPIA PAPERBACK EDITION

Copyright © Sharon Salomon 2023
Illustrations © Muhammed Salah

A CIP catalogue record for this title is
available from the British Library.

ISBN: 978-1-80439-307-9

This is a work of fiction.
Names, characters, places and incidents originate from the writer's
imagination. Any resemblance to actual persons, living or dead, is
purely coincidental.

First Published in 2023

Olympia Publishers
Tallis House
2 Tallis Street
London
EC4Y 0AB

Printed in Great Britain

Dedication

This book is dedicated to all who have embraced their pain and fears, and those who wish to do so, for without it we cannot fully love.

Acknowledgements

Thank you to my angel friend Nikki, for your constant love and encouragement. Thank you, Ima. Thank you to my loved ones who have supported me in my healing and spiritual journey. With love for the Bubble. Here's to hugs filled with enough love to melt broken pieces back together.

Bare Skinned

Bare-skinned I've crawled, raw hand, scraped knee,
Through shards of broken heart,
They've sliced and splintered flesh and bones,
Always of me a part.

Bare-skinned I've crawled, stomach to ground,
Through shards of broken dreams,
Scooped & swallowed the sharpest ones
Unraveling me at the seams.

Bare-skinned I've crawled on hallowed ground,
I learned to pray, deep in the mire,
On bended knee, they've held and shown me
Hope, rebirth, love, desire.

Should I remove shards from my bones,
From splintered burning skin,
Would I space make, would I come home,
A new life to begin?

Wounds

How these wounds ache and wail in pain,
To show me that they're there.
Otherwise, how would I know,
To show them loving care?

Hold on

My solar plexus knew you are bad,
So did my lungs and throat.
My second-guessing, rational mind,
Did keep our love afloat.

Wed

The Best Day of Your Life they say,
In many ways it was true,
I made a perfect perfect day,
But all I wanted was you.

Baby

If you had come right through me,
If you had made it through,
What kind of boy would you be?
Would your favourite colour be blue?

Would your hair be bouncy curls?
Would you love animals too?
Thank you for coming to show me,
Just how much I would love you.

Best Friend

Your eyes dart around this room,
You're about to leave me too soon.

My fingers fold your velvet ear,
You hear me whisper *do not fear.*

I will see you again one day,
And we will run free and play.

I rest my lips upon your face,
You'll ascend now from this place.

Eye to eye, we take your last few breaths,
And then I die a thousand deaths.

Relate

I give
    You take
I fix
    You break,

I leave
    You fear
I grow
    You reappear,

    You harass
I refuse,
My love
    You abuse,

My joy
    You hate,
My heart
    You'll never relate.

Forgive

Now I am to forgive the worst,
Give peace and let you be,
It's for my peace that chords I cut,
As now I am for me.

It was not okay, won't ever be,
But free I choose to live,
Gifts I receive as I let go,
Hence it means *for to give*.

Farewell.

Disappear

If I could choose one place on earth,
Where to forever be,
It's in the forest's rustling heart,
Engulfed by magic trees.

Bubbling

The jagged edges of my Self
rest upon your shoulder,
Your beating heart beside my ear
is heat melting the solder.

Although I know inside this life,
to you I must not tether,
With warmth and strength, you hug and squeeze
My pieces back together.

Think

You are better than you think you are,
Seek feedback, you're also worse,
You are also not your thoughts, it's said,
The mind's balance act curse.

What am I?

Be held to behold

I stand before you, unbolted,
With shaking hands, I know I've faltered,
With racing heart and liquid thighs,
And promises behind your eyes.

My flushed face with strong hands you stroke,
Fires with soft lips you stoke,
I unfurl as to all wounds you tend,
My yearning, fearful heart you mend.

Choice

I don't want to hurt you,
I'd be always filled with regret.
Oh, but my love, you already have,
We just haven't arrived there yet.

Dog

If you are really lucky,
As you wade through a fog,
You will be held and healed,
By the pure love of a dog.

Forest

I immerse myself in lushness,
Here I melt myself away.
Piece by piece this broken heart
In nature finds its way.

Intundla

There's no good way
to quite relay,
Africa's sights, its sound.

The sky performs
Colour soirees,
Bug orchestras abound.

Crickets swoon
This end of day,
This lake's dreams engulf this ground.

These lush trees and I
Can safely say,
Right here magic is found.

Arrested

I want to love,
to yearn, to feel,
to have, to hold,
Moments I steal.

A sensual touch,
A soft caress,
A glance, locked gaze,
A body's arrest.

I want to love,
to yearn, to feel,
Your hands, your weight,
Your electric zeal.

Dew

I present myself to you,
As the rain presents a rose.
Drops of dew wetten for you,
For its love to expose.

Confess

A quickened heart,
Behind this dress,
Like me, it falls for you,
        I confess.

Dreams

A great, old house with ceilings high,
a ballroom and a library,
Grounds and trees and space to fly
and benign ghosts beside me.

These are the places
which hold life and death alike in dreams,
I wish to make this house my home,
my own imprint to leave.

Died

What was that day to be for me?
A tense hug as I rushed by,
A confusing, strange exchange
Before you left this life without *goodbye*.

Surviving, still to be with me,
Shocked to find yourself awake,
Did you see the last years with me,
As some cosmic mistake?

I tore up sealed letters you'd left,
For there was no death here,
But I was wrong, something did die,
It's inside each black tear.

House

Our house is gone,
They took it away.
Can we please have
One last day to play?

Our house is gone,
There's no more time.
Furniture prints and dust,
Where is all that's mine?

Crevices

Breathe loud, slow, and deeply,
Rainbow colours in your vision,
And from crevices of the spirit,
You shall shake loose intuition.

Heal

Healing and wellness
    do not come to be
From sponsored studies or charts.

They're found in the strange,
    eternal caverns
Right inside of our very hearts.

Gratefully Mine

I'm grateful for this morning light,
Leaves rustling in the breeze,
I'm also grateful for my plights,
When broken on my knees.

I'm grateful for music of birds,
The smell of morning dew,
Sunrise, sunset, and magic spells
Even for hell that I've crossed through.

I'm grateful for our human touch,
For sensual ecstasy,
For butterflies, a lover's hug,
Love's exquisite pain and mystery.

I'm grateful for the impossible ways
In which I came to be,
For how inside my very breath
My ancestors are in me.

My Gerbera Flower

In desperate pain, I watch you fall
Pollen by pollen, cell by cell,
Held up in board and precious vase,
I hold weightlessness beyond its hell.

They smell of death, but somehow float
These playful, airborne seeds,
I try to gather them together,
One solid pile for my needs.

They stay moments, present themselves,
And show me they're okay,
No longer they resent themselves,
They want to go, and play.

Suddenly they're beautiful,
Those which neatly come apart,
Their old smell and colour do exist,
Always imprinted in my heart.

Suddenly potential life and love,
To unfurl and fly they strive,
Only when we let them go,
Again they come alive.

Mama

Oftentimes it isn't real,
We shut down what's too much to feel.

Yet there is freedom, there is peace,
You're in the wind stroking the trees.

You're in the patter of the rain,
You're the air holding my pain.

I hate when you permission give,
For me to let go and just live.

But for you, I find joy, colour... glee,
As I know that's what you need from me.

Hug Grief

For those whose loved ones are above,
It helps to remember,
Hug grief as expression of love,
It brings the souls together.

Repentance

Tonight, we start a Holy Fast,
they say it's about Repentance,
Please let me live another year!
we say in Fear and Reverence.

But it's not fear nor beating hearts
which shall keep us alive.
It's how we choose to love ourselves,
be free, not just survive.

Repentance means Forgiveness,
literally "for to give",
Only real Openness and Love,
will have us truly live.

Exist

Death is not only the moment
the soul the body leaves,
It's the colourless life-tapestry
our fears, resentments, weave.

Heart Service

This time
I repent to me.
Make it conscious
so I see,
the horrid words
I've said to me,
    not good enough,
    you failed, you see…

There, there, now child,
inner me…
I love you,
I am so sorry.
I'll hold you,
cry it out, baby.
I'm clearer now,
please forgive me.

Hand on heart,
breath in mind,
eyes closed, I smile
    you're good, you're kind
Hand on heart,
breath in mind,
I tingle, I giggle
    I am good, I am kind.

Ceremony

If you'd knocked on my door last night,
You'd not have found me here.
I flew away, right through the sky,
Ancestral stars shone clear.

We prayed, we danced, we saw and broke
Communal ceremony,
Re-entered as clear canvas,
On purpose, fully free.

Observance

There is a potent moment,
Between each part of your breath,
It is potent **poten**tial,
It is neither life nor death.

A portal, this tiny dot,
To beyond this place,
A momentary connection,
The veil lifts inside this space.

Your angels show you,
We are here,
You see now
You are free and clear.

Here, and so there,
You're not alone,
Take this with you,
When you go home.

Observe this dot,
Between each part of your breath,
Infinity,
Neither life nor death.